Speech Of Poetry

Book Of Poems

OTIS LEE HINTON

authorHOUSE®

AuthorHouse™
1663 Liberty Drive
Bloomington, IN 47403
www.authorhouse.com
Phone: 1-800-839-8640

First published by AuthorHouse   01/17/2012

ISBN: 978-1-4685-4517-3 (sc)
ISBN: 978-1-4685-4516-6 (ebk)

Library of Congress Control Number: 2012901058

Printed in the United States of America

Any people depicted in stock imagery provided by Thinkstock are models, and such images are being used for illustrative purposes only.
Certain stock imagery © Thinkstock.

This book is printed on acid-free paper.

CONTENTS

"Any Enterprise is built by wise planning, becomes stronger through common sense, and profit wonderfully by keeping abreast of the facts." (Prov. 24:3-4)

INTRODUCTION

Although there are many kinds of Poems classified in part according to Style, subject matter, form, intended effect, purpose, metrical pattern and point of view. There are three(3) major divisions of Poetry acknowledged in Western Literature Narrative, Dramatic and Lyric.

Poetry is the oldest form of Literature, and the first too be put into written form. An extremely complex and subjective concept. Poetry cannot be completely or precisely defined. However, it is generally agreed, that Poetry in a literary form expresses, through extraordinary use of language, and a highly developed artistic form, as well as a unique and imaginative interpretation 'of any subject. Good Poetry creates an emotional impact and aesthetical effect by appealing to its Readers Senses and Emotions.

For example: Mary had a little lamb, its fleece was white as show . . . are both lyrical and metrical!!! However, it does not represent the depth of THOUGHT in Ones IMAGINATION… In-hominy with the Mind-Set of Meditation, Relation & Concentration based on the Emotional-feelings which characterizes Real and True Poetry.

My personal philosophical-concept of Real & True Poetry is as follows:

UNCLE OT {POET WITH AN ATTITUDE

As a Poet with an Attitude the beginning of my journey is now told; Speech Of Poetry is the title and format used in My Book of Poems poetically composed.

Its Contents reveals bona-fide real-life situations; based on genuine-feelings, emotions, dispositions and mannerism through the Spoken Words donations.

Articulated too captivate YOUR attention with my Principles of Knowledge, Wisdom & Understanding delivered from each POEM for YOUR reading & listening pleasure as well; entertaining YOUR MIND, BODY & SOUL sincerely Too Show & Tell.

SPECIAL DEDICATION

Speech Of Poetry—Book Of Poems—are dedicated too some very Special People thereof my Life's Self Achievements . . . With TRUE LOVE generating from KINGDOM OF MY HEART; TOO SHOW &TELL MY FATHER & MOTHER, I STILL LOVE THEM IN THE NAME OF GOD:

OWNE HINTON

. . . My Father, Lord God, who planted His-seed
with godly-deeds, and watched it grow; Fatherly, for 12-years, this I Know!!!

MOLLY HINTON-GAVIN

. . . My Mother, Lord-Goddess, who gave BIRTH—Beard-Witness and NURTURED HER SEED for (8) Years DEVOTEDLY; with HER EYES and HEART filled with TEARS & FEARS MOTHERLY!!!

OTIS LEE HINTON

AKA: Guilah Otibah Dikah Habri
Uncle OT {poet with an attitude}
January 2, 1947 (first-birth) 2:am
January 2, 1974 (new-birth) 2:am

FOOD FOR THOUGHT

Our Universal Father Lord God Jehovah Yahweh-Allah-Buddha in the Person of Jesus Christ the Living-god OUR UNIVERSAL MINDS: Controls Life-On-Life's Terms 100% In-Time & In-Space; giving all Creations 90% Free-Will; (Something essential and important for the continual existence for living (one-day-at-a-time)) Here & Now; for generations to come!!!

Every Element in the Universe—Air, Fire, Water, Earth, etc., depends on how YOU & I uses our worldly affairs—Positive or Negative—base on the Temptations for Survival Of The Fittest; yesterday, today and tomorrow!!!

Our Universal-Mind(s)—Super-Conscious; Sub-Conscious & Consciousness—with God-in-Mind . . . preserves 10% of the Kingdom for operating under the Divine Principles with the Laws of Faith, Hope & Love!!! Prescribed as Courses Of Action too be acknowledged & followed daily.

UNIVERSAL PRINCIPLE(S):

(Self Conduct)

1. Knowledge
2. Wisdom
3. Understanding
4. Culture
5. Power
6. Equality
7. God
8. Build & Destroy
9. Birth/Born

. . . Collectively with the 7—seven Principles for the Nguzo Saba doing the period of KWANZAA:

1. Unity (UMOJA)
2. Self Determination (KUJICHAGULIA)
3. Collective Work & Responsibility (UJIMA)
4. Cooperative Economics (UJAMAA)
5. Purpose (NIA)
6. Creativity (KUUMBA)
7. Faith (IMANI)

- TO HEAR THE TRUTH
- TO SEE THE LIGHT
- TO KNOW THE WAY

. . . Requires OUR undivided ATTENTION One For All & All For One!!! Through the SPOKEN WORDS of Silent & Listen respectively: TOO THY OWNSELF BE TRUE!!!

otishinton@ymail.com
609 533-0288
609 532-4865

BUILD ME A-SELF

God, build me a-self, o'lord, who will be strong enough to know when I am weak, brave enough to face myself when I am afraid.

God, build me a-self, o'lord, who will be proud and unbending in honest defeat, humble and gentle in victory.

God, build me a-self, whose wish-bone will not be where my back-bone should be, and I will know thee, and will also know myself, the true-foundation of true-self-knowledge, created in the image and likeness of my God, too-my-own-self-be-true, a-true-living-god!!!

God, I pray, you will not lead me in the path of ease & comfort, but under the stress, spur and hard-work; so that when I am older & wiser, I will not depart from my ways!!! My mind is at peace!!!

God, I pray here, you will let me learn to stand-up in the storm, so that I will know love & compassion for those who failed in their efforts.

God, build me a-self, whose mind & heart will be clear, my goals will be high, who will be master of myself before seeking to master other men.

A-self, who will learn to laugh, yet, never forget how to weep, one, who will reach into the future, yet, never forget the past. God, after all these Principles are mines, I pray, I will have enough sense of humor, so that I will always be serious, yet, never take myself too seriously.

God, also give me humility, so that I will always remember the simplicity of true greatness, an open-mind of true-wisdom and the meekness of true-strength.

God, then You—My Father Lord God Jehovah-Yahweh-Allah-Buddha, in the person of Jesus Christ, the living-god, my Universal-Mind . . . Will dare too whisper; you my-child, have not lived in-vain, I your God, have fulfilled my promise for building you a-self, in my image, after my likeness, and, in my Holy-name; too thy own-self be true . . .

Amen

MY ATTITUDE IN THE SPIRIT

When I awaken each morning with a new vitality I've never known before, my vigor increase, my enthusiasm rises and my desire too greet the world over comes every fear I've known at sunrise; in the Spirit of my God, Super-Consciously.

With my head held-high, in the Spirit of my God, my actions and attitude will always reflect positivity in my gods-mind; in the Spirit of my God, Sub-Consciously.

My physical-appearance, in the Spirit of my God, will always reveal my positive and mental attitude toward life; in the Spirit of my gods-body, Consciously.

My straight and cheerful manner of walking, in the Spirit of my God, will exemplify the positive direction my life has taken; in the Spirit of my gods'-body, Physically.

My eloquent manner of talking, in the Spirit of my God, will always relate the positive, mental, spiritual and physical forces that reside within me; in the Spirit of my gods' body, Vocally.

My illustrious smile, in the Spirit of my God, will always express the pleasure I receive from living; in the Spirit of my gods-body, Facially.

With the positive look in my eyes, in the Spirit of my God, therefore, will always indicate the Self Confidence and the Positive Spirits that lives within me as well; in the Spirit of my god's mind, body & soul godly—I Must Tell.

SHOW & TELL

The year was 1953; when my dearly Beloved Mother taught me. A Poem I recite everyday; too express my compassionate Love for my Parents to say: I loved my Mother dearly, she was motherly as can be; she thought so many hours she worried over me.

My feelings for my Beloved Father, I loved him just as well; the Love I have for my Mother & Father, is Show & Tell. At this time, I was only six(6) years old; years later, my story of True Love, is now told. I dedicate my Poem of Love, with words Spoken from the Kingdom of my Heart; too Show & Tell my Father & Mother, I still LOVE THEM, in the Name of God!!!

Every Tree God creates bear its own fruit; as a by-product of your seeds Mamma & Popper, from Birth, your loving ways have instilled in me, Positive pursuits.

Thank You Mamma & Popper, for your godly Blessings; your teachings on how to become a better Man-Child, with True-Love, have taught me this Lesson.

Too strive in your shadows, too Show & Tell others; the importance for us to learn how to Love one another as Sisters & Brothers.

No mountain is too high, no valley is too low; when it's about True Love, there is no places, Love cannot go . . . Can I get A Witness? SHOW & TELL.

WHO AM I

Who am I? Who am I? Whooo ammm I?! I know I'm not you, you know you aren't me; you and I together are in-search of our true-identity. Who am I? It's written that I was created in the image & likeness of God; these Words of Wisdom I will never discard. Who am I?

As a child I was taught with loving hearts; from the Kingdom within myself this path of righteousness from my childhood, I will never depart. Who am I?

Am I just another guy; sitting among the twelve (12) Apostles at the last suppers fish fry? Who am I?

Where do I go from here; I don't know where I'm truly from, when will I know when I am near? Who am I?

My history knowledge about my Family Tree; must be the key, too set me free, from this state of ignorance godly. Who am I?

Answers to my questions seem too linger on; my need of directions is from you my God, too discover my thorn. Who am I?

Is it really true, I was created in Your Likeness & Imagery; or, is this just another Crime committed by Man called Forgery? Who am I?

Teach your child with a loving-heart; the Kingdom of True Love from within yourself, the Path of Righteousness, your child will never depart . . . Who Are You?

WHEN YOU GOT LOVE

When you got Love, I said, when you got Love, you have everything; that will make your heart sing. Are you an Atheist who do not know about Love; most of your life was lived as a thug?

Are you a person with a cold heart; you never received Love as a child, from the start?

When you got Love, I said, when you got Love, you have everything; too hear Love's bell ring.

Love is that Supreme Power that created Man; one of Gods' Divine Creations, created by hand.

Are you homeless without a place too stay; no-bed too sleep-in, no-pillow for your head too lay; true-love was never sent your way!!!

Remember, when you got Love today; you have Love in every way!!!

Are you lonely without a true-friend indeed; you can't find help from anyone when you are in-need?!

Again remember, when you got self-Love, you got it all; true Love coming from your heart, makes you Stand Tall.

Are you a weak person, young or old; who have adopted Alcohol & Drugs too morally support your Soul?

Who have lost interest in Education too help you know; now you are without Inspirational Knowledge too make your Faith, Hope & Love Grow.

When you got Love, you are never alone; true Love expressed from the Kingdom of your HEART, makes every House Your Home . . . Cause you have L.O.V.E., You Have LOVE!!!

CRACK THE WHITE-SMOKE OF DEATH

Greetings Brothers & Sisters!!! Today, I wish too share with you's a Poem about one of the most deadliest Drugs in our World; raising its gas-like vapors too destroy this Generation of Our Young Boys & Girls!!!

My Poem is based on a Dream, I had some time ago; its A poem about a Dream, but, don't get it mixed-up, this character CRACK, some of you's might know?!

In my Dream, I was on my way too work; I stepped into this building with a sign hanging on its wall that read—CRACK HOUSE WELCOME JERK!!!

In this room I saw a strange object talking to a group of EARS; I realized that this object was a CHEMICAL called CRACK—a deadly DRUG used by some People too get HIGH—for trying too ESCAPE their FEARS!!!

CRACK said: "I came to this Country without a Legal-Passport; every since then, I have been Preserved in-Salt. My little White-Grains is nothing but WASTE; that's soft & deadly, and bitter too TASTE.

So, be YOU—ITALIAN, JEWISH, BLACK OR MEX; I can make the most MACHOS OF MEN, forget THEIR SEX!!!

Now, my FELLOWMAN, you must do your best; too keep-up your HABITS until YOUR MIND, BODY & SOUL are at rest!!! Now that the Police have taken You from under my Wing; do you think they deny me WHO IS KING? You must lay in the County Jail; where I cannot get too you by VISIT or MAIL!!! As You SQUIRM, WRIGGLE & COUGHT; six(6) days of MADNESS, you just might through me off!!! Curse me in-name, defy me in-speech; you know, you will pick-me-up-right-now, if I was in YOUR REACH!!! All through your CENTERS, as you become dissolved in YOUR FAITH; fear not YOUNG MAN or WOMAN, I will be waiting at the Gate. Don't be AFRAID, don't RUN, I Will Not Chase; sure my name is CRACK—The White-Smoke Of Death!!! It's just a matter of time, before YOU, come back to me for another TASTE!!! You are HOOKED!!! Your foot-is-on the-gas—make-haste-over-the-mountains—drive your-vehicle-well: for me CRACK—The White-Smoke Of Death!!! Will Drive You Too Hell!!! Too Hell!!! I Will Drive You Too Hell!! ! Young Man or Woman—Until You Is Dead!!!

LETTER FROM SATAN

Greetings Sinners!!!

"This is just a Letter of appreciation, from me to you; I like to say Thanks for letting me use You for most of your life, over & over and through & through . . . You are so gullible: I saw you yesterday, as you begin your daily chores, when you awoke without kneeling too Pray; this really made my day!!!

As a matter of fact, you did not even bless your meal, or Pray, before going to bed last night. You are so un-thankful!!!

I cannot tell you how glad, I am that you decided to go another day without giving your Life & Will to God; I do not understand why your head is so-hard!!! I am glad, however, that you have not changed your Ways of living, in due-time; you will be mine!!! Remember that you & I have been going-steady for years but I don't Love you; because of what Your God have put me through!!! As a matter of fact, I hate you because I hate your God!!! I am only using you too get even with God. He kicked me out of Heaven!!! I am going to use you for as long as possible to pay Him back!! ! You see your God Loves you, and He has some great Plans for you!!! But you have yielded your Life too me!!! I am going to make your Life a living Hell!!! This way, you and I will be together twice; ant that nice???

This will really hurt God, thanks to you. I am really showing Your God whose boss in your Life today . . . With all the good-times You & I have had—watching dirty-movies; cussing folks out; partying everyday; stealing; lying; hypocriting; fornicating; smoking crack; drugging & drinking; working roots; telling dirty jokes; gossiping & backstabbing people . . . come-on, lets burn together forever, I have some hot plans for us!!! Well, I must go now, but I will be back in a few seconds to tempt you again ok.

If you are really smart, you will run somewhere and Confess Your Sins and Live for Your God. With what little bit of Life You have left!! ! You know it's not in my true nature to warn any-body, right!!! But to be your age, and still Sinning has become a bit ridiculous—what do you think??? If you really love-me, you will not share this letter with any-one, today or tomorrow!!! Hate Satan!!!"

IN THE SPIRIT I MEDITATE

I Meditate in the Spirit; in the Spirit I Meditate too find recession from Life's weariness, restlessness and displeasures, so that my SOUL can catch its breath and restore its scattered strength; I Meditate in the Spirit!!!

In the Spirit I Meditate too find Peace from the disorders and lack of harmony; from the tensions and turmoil of coping with Life's chores & challenges in my Society; I Meditate in the Spirit!!!

In the Spirit I Meditate too see Life steadily and see it whole; so that whatever I experience, I can absorb and relate to my visions in Life and place it in its proper perspective double-fold; I Meditate in the Spirit!! !

In the Spirit I Meditate so that my surface Life, and my interior Life be not at odds with one another; but are mutually reinforced, and brought into harmony & oneness like a brother; I Meditate in the Spirit!!!

In the Spirit I Meditate too discover the depths of my TRUE NATURE, by discovering and releasing the forces hidden there-in the reserves of strength & endurance; with the POWER of self-recovery & self-healing, that waits upon my quite bidding through PERFORMANCE; I Meditate in the Spirit!!!

In the Spirit I Meditate to become fully alive & fully human who is aware of the I-in-Me, me-in-other-people—knowing none-of-us is an ISLAND—YOU & ME TOGETHER are parts of the MAIN; the bells that tolls-for you—is-tolling-for-me, just the same; I Meditate in the Spirit!!!

In the Spirit I Meditate too better grasp the meaning of My Human existence, and my OWN PURPOSE with meaningful PRINCIPLES upon this EARTH; so that I can mine the hidden-treasures of living Life-On-Life's Terms, and be sustained by the LESSONS LEARNED FROM MY BIRTH; I Meditate in the Spirit!!!

In the Spirit I Meditate to sift the wheat from the rubbish values in my Society; so that I can adhered to the essential, and gladly let the trivial go freely; I Meditate in the Spirit!!! IN THE SPIRIT I MEDITATE; I MEDITATE IN THE SPIRIT OF MY GOD TOO EDUCATE.

MARRIAGE BEFORE THE CEREMONY

God said: "Let's make Man in Our Image & Likeness;" God therefore, created the Universe & Man-Kind in Righteousness. Marriage Before The Ceremony.

God then bestowed Man with a Mind, Body & Soul; gifts, rewards & Blessings from God, too make ALL CREATIONS WHOLE. Marriage Before The Ceremony.

God then gave Man-Kind Free-Will; when ever ANY CREATION is Tempted for ANY RIGHT or WRONG REASON—MAN-KIND in HIS or HER Better Judgment Must Foot-One's-Own Bill!!! Marriage Before The Ceremony.

God then afforded EVERY SPECIES and/or HUMAN-KIND an opportunity for a Family; where ALL SPECIES would Learn & Understand each other through the Principle of Collective Work & Responsibility. Marriage Before The Ceremony.

God then presented MANKIND with WAYS & MEANS too COMMUNICATE; where every Species would teach beloved ONES how to prosper, succeed & congregate. Marriage Before The Ceremony.

God then inscribed Universal Principles for Man too build upon His & Her godlike characters for Self Conduct; Knowledge, Wisdom, Understanding, Culture, Power, Equality, God, Build & Destroy & Born/Birth—too be acknowledged in OUR ACTIONS & ATTITUDES and not SELF DESTRUCT. Marriage Before The Ceremony.

God, again, said: "I The Creator of the Heavens, the Earth and the Universe—One for All & All for One—pronounce Yon My Children, My Husband & My Wife; until Death do You apart from Me For Life." Marriage Before The Ceremony.

TIFFANY

My dearly beloved Tiffany, Tiffany, Tiffany Delight; your modeling debut embraces you so romantically bright.

This day, I greet you with love in my heart; in-spite of us living so-far apart. Your illustrious smile and exotic sex appeal bubbling from the pages of our favored magazine; have provoked my heart Tiffany to desire you as my Queen. I act now, too apprehend a chance for us too meet; before I lost this opportunity forever in defeat.

Your Love, will mean the greatest secret toward our success; assuring you & I together, in oneness, a life-time of happiness. My boo Tiffany, I am not sure of your expectations in your kind of man; without any doubt, My Love, my goal is to become your Knight-in-shiny-armor, as a friend.

Every drip-drop of your teasing loveliness, comes into my dreams suddenly, suddenly; crying-out your name Tiffany, Tiffany!!!

When I look upon your lovely picture baby, I am reborn-again; obsessed with feelings of wanting to hug, touch & kiss you, My Love, without end!!!

In closing my letter, remember always my goddess of the universe, if we have no other qualities, we can succeed with Love alone; for now and evermore, it is with you Ms. Tiffany Delight, whom I wish to share My Throne.

LETTER FROM JESUS

My Dearly Beloved Precious Friend!!!

"I am sending you this Letter by-way of One of My Disciples: Herein My Message, I just wanted to let you know how much, I truly Love & Care about You!!! And, how I greatly Desire to become a meaningful-part, in Your Life!!!

This Morning, when you awoke, I was already there with you, in the light of my beautiful Sun-Shine that filled your Room. I was hoping that You would say Good Morning to Me!!! You didn't!!! So I thought maybe, it was just a little too early in-the-day for you to notice!!!

Again, I tried to get your attention, when you stepped-out-of-the-door . . . I Kissed Your Face with a soft-gentle-breeze!!! I then sang You—A Love Song—through the Birds in the Trees!!! But You just walked right-past Me!!!

However, later on in the Day, I watched over-you!!! as you were talking with some of your Friends!!! OH!!! How I wished that you would talk-too-Me-as-well!!! I waited & waited!!! but, you just went along-your way!!!

This afternoon, I sent you a refreshing Shower, and a glistened a-two from each Rain-drop!!! I even shouted-to-you with My Thunder—trying to get your attention!!! then I Painted you a lovely Rainbow in the midst of my fluffy White Clouds!!! I just knew you would see Me then!!! But you were unaware of My presence!!!

This Evening, too close your Day, I sent you a beautiful Sun Set!!! After that, I winked at you a thousand times through My Stars!!! Hoping, that you would Wink-back!!! You never did!!!

To-Night, when you went to Bed, I spilled some Moon Light upon your Face, too let you know, I was still there with you!!!

Then, I was hoping that you would Talk to Me a little while before you went to Sleep!!! You never said a Word!!!

It hurt Me deeply, however, I continued to watch-over-You all through the Night!!! Thinking—that maybe just maybe you would call My Name sometime throughout the Night!!!

Each and Everyday, I have revealed Myself too You in many strange &. wonderful ways!!! Hoping that you would Accept Me, as Your Shepherd?! For I am the Only One that can Supply You with All Your humanly NEEDS!!! My Love for You is deeper than the deepest Ocean & bigger than the great Blue Sky!!! I have so very much too Give You; also, to Share with You!!!

PS: Please let Me hear from You!!!
YOUR LOVING FRIEND FOREVER!!!
LORD GOD JESUS CHRIST"

GREATEST LOVER IN THE UNIVERSE

Today, our Father Lord God Jehovah-Yahweh-Allah-Buddha have prepared for us a new way; in the person of Jesus Christ—the living god—our universal-mind, to say:

Shed your old-skin; live by the spirit of your godly soul, within. For too long, you have suffered the bruises of failure, and the wounds of handicap as your spouse; the dawn of a new day is upon you, too thy own-self be true, believe in your abilities for building your-self, a better house. Greatest Lover In The Universe.

Your birth-place is the vine-yard in the world; where the fruits from your labor will benefit the next generation of young boys & girls. Pluck grapes of wisdom from your spiritual growth, and material-gains; planted by the wisest of your ancestors, for your claim too-fame. Greatest Lover In The Universe.

Save these tastes of grapes, from each vine, and swallow the seeds of success buried in each; where new-life will spout within you, for others to reach, as you teach. Greatest Lover In The Universe.

The career you have chosen is lading with opportunity, yet, fraught with heart-breaks, despairs and bodies of those who have failed; they are piled one-on-top of each other, in-cells. Greatest Lover In The Universe.

I EMBRACE TODAYWITH

LOVE IN MYHEART

Today I Embrace this Day with Love in My Heart; the greatest secret of success in all ventures by for. Muscles can split shields and even destroy life; only the unseen power of love can open the hearts of men without strife.

Hence until I master this art of love I will remain no more than a peddler in the market place; I will make love my greatest tool and, none whom I call upon can defend against its grace.

Hence my reasoning they may not understand; my speech of poetic justice may upset their plan.

My plans for cooperative economics they may distrust; after they review my objectives consistent with their own they all will agree it is a must.

My godlike appearance may cause suspicion; with a bright friendly smile of love on my face will reflect on our tradition.

My love will melt all hearts; just as the Sun-rays soften the coldest day like God.

I Embrace this Day with Love in My Heart:

How will I approach my Chores based on Lifes' Terms?
I will look upon all Manners of Nature with Love and I will be Re-born:
I will Love the Sun for it warms my bones;
I will Love the Rain for it cleans my spirit;
I will Love the Light for it shows me the way;
I will Love the Darkness for it reveals the stars to me;
I will welcome Happiness for it enlarges my Heart.
Yet I will endure Sadness for it opens my Soul.
I will acknowledge all people places and things in Nature for they are my just due.
I will also frown on obstacles for they are my challenge too.

I Embrace this Day with Love in My Heart:

How will I respond to all My Challenges?
I will applause my Enemies and they will become my Friends.

I will encourage my Friends and they will become my sisters, brothers and children.
I will always look for reasons to Love, Honor, Respect and Praise others never will I scratch for excuses to gossip and backstab them in sin.

Hence when I am moved to Praise I will Shout for the Root: When I am tempted to criticize I will bite on my tongue. Is it not True that all of Nature and its Elements speak with music of Praise to their Creator? Cannot I the Greatest Lover in the World communicate with God's children with the same tune? I will always remember this profound principle and it will enhance my godlike character and change my life forever.

I Embrace this Day with Love in My Heart:

Hence, how will I react to all Temptations in my Worldly Affairs? I will Love all Manners of Mankind because each has qualities to be admired even though they are hidden. With Love I will tear down the walls of suspicion and hate which they have built around their Hearts. In its place I will build bridges of Love so that My Love will enter their Souls with Peace.

I Embrace this Day with Love in My Heart:

I will Love the ambitious for they can inspire me;
I will Love the failurers for they can teach me;
I will Love the Kings for they are but human;
I will Love the Meek for they are divine;
I will Love the Wealth for they are yet lonely;
I will Love the Poor for they are so many;
I will Love the Young for the Faith they hold;
I will Love the Old for the Wisdom they share;
I will Love the Beautiful for their eyes of sadness; yet,
I will Love the Ugly for· their Souls of Peace.

I Embrace this Day with Love in My Heart:

How will I act and react to the actions from others?
With knowledge, wisdom, understanding, peace, honor, respect and Love. Just as Love is a weapon to open the Hearts of men. Love is also my Shield to repulse the arrows of hate, the spears of anger, adversity and discouragement from others without end. That will beat against my New Tool for protection and become the softest of rain.

Hence, my Shield of Love will protect me in the market, place and sustain my life in balance in moments of despair. Yet, it will also clam me in times of excitement. My New Instrument becomes stronger and more sustaining with use. Until one day I will cast it aside and walk unafraid among all Manners of my fellow men eternally; as a result, my name will be placed on the Pyramids of Life for all too See.

I Embrace this Day with Love in My Heart:

Hence, how will I share my Spiritual Teachings with those whom I meet?
The perpetuation of my Lessons will shine in my eyes from my old-school knowledge. Universal studies learned from personal sacrifice, charity and self-control of my actions and attitude of becoming godlike. By unwrinkling my eyebrows, bring a smile to my lips, an echo in my voice, and opening the Hearts of all men with cries from the Love I Share. Then, who will there be to say nay to my Goodness when their Hearts feels my Love?

I Embrace this Day with Love in My Heart:

Hence, today I Love My 'God unconditionally.
Today, I Love Myself godly.

Today, I zealously inspect all things that enters my Mind, my Body, my Heart and my Soul righteously.

Today, I never allow my Mind to be attracted to evilness and despair. Rather, I uplift my godly mind with knowledge and wisdom from the legacy of my Ancestors.

Today, I will never over indulge in the requests of my flesh. Rather, I cherish my Body with cleanliness and moderation.

Today, I never allow my Heart to become small and bitter. Rather, I cultivate my Heart with Seeds of Love so that it will grow and warm the Earth with glitter.

Today, I never allow my Soul to become complacent and dis-satisfied. Rather, I feed my Soul with Meditation and Prayer.

I Embrace this Day with Love in My Heart:

Today, I Love all of Humanity. From this moment Hate is drained from my Vains. I have no time for Animosity only time for Love.

Today, I take the first step required to become a better and wiser person among my Fellow Men godly. With Love I will increase my reputation a hundred folds as the Greatest Lover in the World.

Today, if I have no other qualities I can succeed with Love alone. Without Love I will fail like others. Even though I possess much knowledge, wisdom and understanding about living life on life-terms. And many talents and skills for changing most of the negative conditions in my environment.

Today I Embrace this Day with Love in My Heart; I will Succeed with Love for My God.

I Embrace This Day With Love In My Heart:

I WILL ENDURE UNTIL I SUCCEED

In the Orient young Bulls are tested for the Fight Arena in a certain manner. Each Bull is brought into the Ring and allowed to attack a Picador which picks them with a Lance. The bravery of each Bull is rated with care according to the number of times they demonstrates the willingness to charge inspite of the sting from the blade.

Henceforth, when I recognize that each day I am tested by Life on Life Terms, in the same manner. If I Persist with strong efforts. If I continue to charge forward, I Will Succeed. I wasn't delivered from my birth into this World in defeat. Nor, does Failure course in my veins. I am not waiting to be prodded by a Shepherd. Rather, I prefer to be as a Lion by refusing to talk, walk and sleep with Sheeps.

Hence, I will not listen to those who weep and complain aimlessly for their disease is contagious. I will let ungodly complainers join the weak. The slaughter house of failure is not my destiny.

I will Endure Until I Succeed:

Hence, the Prizes of Life's struggle is at the end of each journey and not near the beginning. As a Child it was not given to me to know how many steps are necessary before reaching my destiny. Failure I may still encounter at my thousandth step.

Yet, Success maybe hidden behind the next bend in the Road. I may never know how close it lies until I turn the next corner. I will always take another step. If that step is of no avail? I will take another yet another step until I Succeed. In truth, one step at a time isn't that difficult.

I Will Endure Until I Succeed:

Henceforth, I will consider each days effort as but one blow of my blade against the mighty Oak. My first blow may not cause a tremor in the Oak. Nor the second or third. Each blow of itself maybe trifling and seem of no consequence. Yet, from childish swipes the Oak will eventually fall.

Hence, so will it be with my efforts of today. I will be like rain drops that washes away the Mountain. The ant who devours the Tiger. The Stars that brightens the Earth. The 24 Grand Style Speech of Poetry Slave who built the Pyramids. I will gather one brick at a time for building my Castle. I know that attempts repeated will complete my undertakings.

I Will Endure Until I Succeed:

Hence I will never consider defeat without struggle. I shall remove these Words from my Vocabulary:
Quit;
Cannot;
Unable;
Impossible;
Failure;
Unworkable;
Hopeless;
Retreat;
Out of the Question!

Hence, these are Words of Fools. I will avoid despair but if this disease should affect me mentally? Then I will work on despair devotedly. I will toil! I will Endure! I will ignore the obstacles at my feet and keep my eyes on the Goals above my Head. I understand where dry deserts end green grass grows.

I Will Endure Until I Succeed:

Hence, I will always remember this Ancient Law of Average and I will bend it to my good. I will persist with positive knowledge and a firm understanding that each failure to exchange my Love will increase my chances for success at my next attempt.

Each day I hear brings me closer to the sound of yea.
Each frown I meet only prepares me for the Smiles to come. Each misfortune I encounter carries with it the seeds of tomorrows good luck. I must appreciate the day to enjoy the night. I must fail often to succeed only once.

I Will Endure Until I Succeed:

Hence, I will try, try and try again. E.ach obstacle I will consider as a mere detour toward reaching my goals and a challenge against my profession. I will persist and develop my skills like the Marine who develops his by learning to ride out the waves from each storm.

I Will Endure Until I Succeed:

Hence, I will Learn how to apply the secrets from those who excels from my teachings. When each day ends and not regarding whether it was a Success or Failure? I will attempt to make yet another Love Connection. Even when my tired Body beckon me homeward, yet, I will resist its temptation to depart and try again.

Hence, never will I allow my days to end in failure. I will plant the seeds for tomorrow's success. Giving me an incredible advantage over those who cease their Labor before it's time to retire. When others arrest their struggle then mine begins and my harvest becomes full.

I Will Endure Until I Succeed:

19

Hence, nor will I allow yesterdays success to pull me into today's complacency. This is one of the greatest foundation of failure. I will forget the happenings of today whether they were good or bad?! Therefore greeting the New Sun Rise with Confidence that this will be the best day of my entire Life.

Hence, as long as there is Breath in my Body that long will I Persist. Today I know one of the Greatest Principles of Success. If I Persist long enough I Will Win. I Will Persist. I Will Win.

I Will Endure Until I Succeed:

I AM HUMANITIES GREATEST MIRACLE

Since the beginning of my birth never has there been another with my mind, body, soul. Nor, with my exact Way of Life. Who think, talk, walk or express themselves as I do:

Hence, all of Mankind is my brothers and sisters, yet, I am different from each. I am a Unique Ingredient of Nature. I am also of the Animal Species Kingdom. But animal rewards alone will not satisfy my nature godly.

Within me burns a flame that was passed down from generations by my Ancestors uncounted. Its heat is a constant irritation to My Soul to become better today, than yesterday. I will fan this flame of dissatisfaction from yesterday, today. And proclaim my uniqueness in the world today and tomorrow.

There is none today, who can duplicate my birth and likeness nor, my creative abilities exactly. In truth, there is none who have the same CHARISMA to exchange Love as I can. Therefore, I will capitalize off this indifference for it is an asset to be promoted to its fullest.

I am Humanities Greatest Miracle:

Hence, vain attempts to pretend I am someone else no longer will I undertake. Instead, I will place my uniqueness on display in the market place. I will pronounce it to the world. I will Love it too.

Lover and loving is different from all other professions. I am proud of my difference professionally. I am a peculiar creature of nature. I am rare, and there is value in rarity. I am better equipped intelligently, emotionally and physically than all the emperors and wise men who proceed me.

Hence, until I employ my mind, body and soul for good use they will stagnant, rot and die. My potentials are unlimited and endless. Only a small portion of my brain do I exercise. Only a fraction on my muscles do I flex.

Hence, a hunder folds or more I can increase my abilities from yesterday and this I will do today. Never will I be satisfied with my accomplishments from yesterday. Nor, will I indulge in deeds for Self Praise. When in reality these Self Praised Deeds are too small for acknowledging wisely. I can achieve far more than I have and I will today, tomorrow and forever more. Why should the Miracle that produced my birth end? I can extend those miracles from yesterday and add them to my deeds for today.

I am Humanities Greatest Miracle:

Hence, I am not on this Earth by chance. I am on Earth for a purpose. My intentions is too grow into a mountain not shrink to a grain of sand. Today, I will exhaust all of my efforts to become the highest mountain on Earth. I will strain my potentials until they cry for Mercy. I will intensify my abilities and increase my Self Knowledge for Loving My God, Myself and Humanity.

Hence, I will Love my God unconditionally. I will share and exchange my Love with my fellow men godly. That will multiply as I practice, polish and improve the Words I utter for sharing my ideas about changing the Things I Can. And accepting the people, places and things I cannot. This is the Foundation I will Build My Career: Crime Anonymous Reformation Prevention. Parents Education All Children Educated. Public Education Americas' Culture Educated. Spiritual Growth Fellowship.

Hence, I will never forget many have obtained Great Wealth and Success with only a few Words delivered in Excellence. Therefore, I will constantly seek ways and means to heal my Mannerism and my Grace. For I Know these are the honey that others are attracted too.

I am Humanities Greatest Miracle:

Hence, I will concentrate my energies on the challenges for the moment. My actions will help me to forget everything else. The problems in my home will remain at home. I will not think of my Family while in the market place. Such thoughts will only cloud my business sense. The problems in the Market Place shall also remain at my place of business. There is no room in the Market Place for Loving My Family nor, is there any room in My Home for during business. I will Divorce one from the other, yet, I will remain wedded to both. Separated they must remain. Or, my Career will die and my Family will be destroyed. This is a Paradox handed down from my Ancestors.

I am Humanities Greatest Miracle:

Hence, I have been blessed with Eyes to See. An Imagination to visualize my hopes, dreams and aspirations for the future. Now I know, I possess an extraordinary Secret and Science about myself godly.

Today, I realize that all my discouragements and heartaches in truth, are splendid opportunities in disguise for Free Will.

Today, the garments they wear will no longer fool me, now days, my Eyes are open. I can see beyond the clothing my adversaries wear to deceive myself and others.

I am Humanities Greatest Miracle:

Hence, no other creation in Humanity had the same beginning as I. I was conceived in Love. Brought forth with a unique purpose here on Earth. In the past, I never considered this as a known Fact. Today, the Truth is the Light. That has come out of darkness to guide and shape my Life with something essential for the continual existence with greater opportunities to Come.

I am Humanities Greatest Miracle:

I WILL ENTERTAIN THIS

DAY LIKE IT IS MY LAST

Today, I will Entertain this Day like it is My Last:

What shall I do with this last day that remains in my keepings? First, I will seal up its container of Life so that not one drop spill itself upon the Earth.

Henceforth, I will not waste a moment mourning over yesterdays misfortunes; yesterdays defeats; yesterdays ashes from the fire:
Why should I throw Good after Bad?
Can Sand flow upward in the hourglass?
Will the Sun rise where it set; set where it rise?
Can I relive the errors from yesterday and right them today?
Can I call back yesterdays wounds and make them whole today?
Can I become younger than yesterday, today?
Can I take back the evil words spoken, the blows struck, the pain caused yesterday and right them today?
No! Yesterday is buried forever and I will think of past bad-incidents or good-deeds that I have no power to change.

I will Entertain this Day like it is My Last:

What shall I do with today?
Forgetting yesterday, neither will I think of Tomorrow.
Why should I throw now after maybe?
Can tomorrows Sand flow through the hourglass before today?
Will the Sun rise twice this morning?
Can I perform tomorrow's deeds while standing in today's path?

Can I place tomorrows gold into today's purse?
Can tomorrow's child be born today?
Can tomorrow's death cast its shadow backward and darken today's joy?
Should I torment myself about problems. that may never come to pass?
No! Tomorrow lies buried with yesterday and I will think of it no more.

I will Entertain this Day like it is My Last:

Hence, this day is all I have and these few hours are now my eternity: I greet this Sunrise with cries of joy as a perished person who is reprieved from death. I lift my arms with thanks for this priceless gift of a new day.

Hence, I beat on my chest with gratitude as I consider all those who greeted yesterdays Sunrise but are not among the living today. I am indeed a blessed person and today's hours are but a bonus underved. Why have I been allowed to live another day, when others far more better than myself have departed?

Hence, is it that they have accomplished their goals while mine is still yet to be achieved? Is this the opportunity for me to become the Greatest Lover in the World? Is there a divine purpose behind all my blessings? Is this my day to excel in my Worldly affairs?

I will Entertain this Day like it is My Last:

Hence, I have but one Life and its nothing but a measurement in-time. When I waste today, I am destroying the last page that represents the final chapter of my entire life from birth. Each hour of this day I will cherish for it can never be replaced. I cannot be banked today and be withdrawn tomorrow. Who can trap the Wind?

Hence, each minute of this day I will grasp with both hands and fondle it with Love. These moments I value is priceless. What dying man can purchase another breath? Though he be willing to give all his life earnings in gold. What price I dare put on the hours ahead? Time is one of the Universe's most precious resources.

I will Entertain this Day like it is My Last:

Hence, I will avoid with fury the killers of Time. Frustration I will destroy with Action. Doubt I will bury under Faith. Fear I will dismember under Confidence.

Hence, where there are idle Mouths I will not Listen. Where there are impractical Hands I will not Linger. Where there are worthless bodies I will not Visit.

Henceforth, I know to court Unemployment is to steal food, clothing and warmth from those I Love dearly. I am not a Thief! Today, is my last chance to prove my Love and my greatness in the world.

I will Entertain this Day like it is My Last:

Hence, if this is my last day on Earth it shall be my greatest moment to build my legacy. This day, I will make the best Day of my entire Life. This day, I will act upon every minute to its fullest. I will save its results and give thanks to my God. I will make every Hour count for something Good. And only Trade something of Value.

Hence, I will Labor harder than ever before by pushing my muscles until they cry for relief I will then continue on my journey of making more Love Calls then ever before. I will then exchange more goodness in the world to influence as many people I can in the History of Mankind.

Hence, I will earn more spiritual, physical and financial rewards then ever before. Each moment of today will be more fruitful than any hour of yesterday. My last must be my best.

I will Entertain this Day like it is My Last:

Hence, if this is not my last Doyon Earth?! I shall Fall To My Knees and Give Thanks To My God for a New Day. Aman.

I Will Entertain This Day Like It Is My Last:

TODO I WILL BE MASTER

OF MY ATTITUDE

The tides advance, the tides recede. Winter goes and the Summer comes. The Heat gets hot and the Cold gets colder. The Sunrise and the Sunsets, the Moon is full and the Moon is dark. The Birds appear and the Birds depart. The Flowers bloom and the Flowers fade, the Seeds are sown and the Harvest is ripen and gathered. Nature is a circle of moods and I am apart of Nature. Like Nature, the tides of my moods will rise and my moods will fall.

Today I will be Master of My Attitude:

Hence, it is one of Nature's tricks that little in known how each Day when I awaken with moods changed from yesterday. Yesterday's joy will become today's sadness. Yet, today's sadness will grow into tomorrow's joy. Inside me is a wheel constantly turning from pleasure to pain, from joy to sadness and from excitement to depression. From happiness to melancholy. Like the Flowers, today's full bloom of joy will fade and wither into a state of despondency. Yet, I will always remember as today's dead Flowers carries the seeds of tomorrow's joy.

Today I will be Master of My Attitude:

Hence, how will I Master My Attitude so that each day will be productive? Unless my moods are right the day will be a Failure. Trees and plants depends on the Rain too flourish, yet, I make my own weather which I transplant with me. If I bring my own rain, gloom, darkness and pessimism no one will favor my goodness of Love.

If I bring my own joy, brightness, enthusiasm and laughter to my family, friends and associates they will react with bliss, gleam, fascination, laughter and happiness. My Weather of Love will produce a harvest of bargains and a grander of Love for me.

Today I Will be Master of My Attitude:

Hence, how will I be Master of My Attitude so that each moment shared with others are happy and good? To Learn is a struggle, yet, to know is Peace of Mind. I have Learned the Secrets of my Ancestors. Weak is those who allows their thinking to control their Actions. E.ach Day I awaken, I will follow this plan of battle before I am imprisoned by the forces of self pity and sadness:

If I feel depressed? I will Sing.
If I feel sad? I will Laugh.
If I feel ill? I will double my Labor.
If I feel fear? I will remember past Challenges.
If I feel uncertain? I will work on building-up my Self Confidence.
If I feel poverty? I will think of wealth to come.
If I feel incompetent? I will remember the significance of my talents and life skills.
If I feel insignificant? I will recall my Goals.

Today I Will be Master of My Attitude:

Hence, I will always remember only those with inferior ability are at their best. Yet, I am not Inferior. There are Days when I must constantly struggle against forces that threatens to tear me down. Forces such as despair and sadness is simple to recognize. But those that approach with smiles and handshakes of friendship can also destroy me. Against these forces I must never relinquish control.

If I become over confidant? I will remember my failures.
If lover indulge in the request of my Flash? I will think of past Affairs.
If I feel complacency? I will recall my Competition.
If lover enjoy moments of greatness? I will Commemorate moments of Shame.
If I feel all powerful? I will Try to Stop the Wind.
If I become overly proud? I will remember moments of Weakness.
If I feel my skills are unmatched? I will Look at the Stars.

Today I Will be Master of My Attitude:

Hence, with my new insight I will recognize and understand the Moods of those whom I call upon for fellowship. I will make allowance for the anger and irritation of today for him and her who don't know the secrets of controlling their Thoughts. Therefore, I will understand their arrows of insults. Now I know that tomorrow they will change and become a joy to approach. No longer will I judge anyone on our first meetings. No longer will I fail to call on them again in the future in spite of our misunderstandings for today.

Today, one may not buy a gold chariot for a penny, yet, tomorrow they will exchange their house for a Tree. My knowledge and understanding of this ancient Secret is the Key to gain great Wealth.

Today I Will be Master of My Attitude:

Hence, I will recognize this Mood of Mystery in all my fellowmen, and above all, I will also identify my own Moods within myself as well. From this moment forth I am prepared to control whatever Moods I awaken with in My Attitude each day.

Hence, each and every Day I will strive to be Master of my Moods through positive action. When I Master my Moods, I will control my own destiny. My Destiny is to become the Greatest Lover in the World.

Today I Will Be Master Of My Attitude:

I WILL SMILE AT THE WORLD

No living creature have been blessed with the gift of Smiles like Man. Trees will bleed when wounded, Beats in the Forest will cry from pain and hunger. Yet, only Man have the gift of Laughter and Smile. My gift and blessings of Laughter and Smile is mine to use whenever I choose.

Hence, I will cultivate this habit of Smiles. When I master this habit of Laughter and Smiles my digestion will improve. When I chuckle my burdens will become lighter. Smiling and laughter is the secret to longer Life. When I Smile my Life is lengthen. Now smiles, laughter and longer Life is mine.

I Will Smile At The World:

Hence, most of all I will laugh at myself Man is most comical when he takes himself too seriously. Never will I fall into this trap of the Mind. Though, I am Humanities Greatest Miracle, I am still a mere grain of sand tossed about by the winds of time.

Hence, do I truly know where I am from? Or, where I am bound? Will not my concerns for this Day's achievements seem foolish in years to come? What can take place before Sunrise, that will seem insignificant in the river of centuries?

Hence, how can I Smile when confronted with negative Insults which offends me? Too bring forth my Tears and Curses? My Grand Style Speech of Poetry Book of Poems constructive Words of Wisdom. I will Train myself to express thoroughly. Until they become a force of habit so strong my Words of positivity will be expressed immediately. That will appear in my memory-bank whenever good humor threatens to depart from my sense of humor. These Words of Wisdom passed down through generations will carry me over, around and through every adversity and maintain my Life in balance.

I Will Smile At The World:

Hence, all Worldly Affairs shall pass with Time. When I am burden with heartaches? I shall tell myself that this to will pass. When I am faced with poverty? I will inform myself that this too shall eventually come to pass.

Hence, where are those who built the Pyramids? Aren't they buried within its Stones? Will not one Day the Pyramids will also be buried under Sand? If all people, places and things shall pass? Why should I trouble myself about situations that will eventually go away as well?

I Will Smile At The World:

Hence, I will paint this Day with Smiles and laughter. I will also frame my Nights with songs, smiles and laughter. Never will I Labor to be happy rather I will remain too busy to be sad. I will enjoy today's Happiness Today.

Hence, it is not for Grains to be stored in a box. It is not for Wine to be saved in a jar. The quality of their Values are for today, that must be sown and ripen on the same day.

This I will do henceforth: With Smiles and Laughter all people, places and things shall be reduced to their True Values:
I will Smile and laugh at my Success and it will shrink to its true size.
I will laugh and Smile at evil and it will die untasted.
I will laugh and Smile at goodness and it will thrive and abound.

Each and every day will only be triumphant when my Smiles bring forth Smiles from others. Then my Harvest will be full. There are Times when I will be Selfish toward those whom I meet for the first time that I will frown upon. Who are basically those who do not accept my goodness in Fellowship.

I Will Smile At The World:

Hence, shedding Tears for those of sadness, romance and frustration is of no Value in the Market Place. While each Smile and Kind Word spoken from the kingdom of My Heart can be exchanged for gold and also build a Castle. Never will I allow myself to become too important; to wise; to dignified or all powerful that I will forget how to laugh and Smile at myself and the World. In this manner I shall always remain as a Child. Only a Child is born with the abilities to lookup with respect to their Elders. I will never grow too long for my Cot.

I Will Smile At The World:

Hence, so long as I can laugh and Smile never will I be Poor. Laughter and Smiles are one of Nature's greatest gifts given to Mankind. I will not waste my godly gifts no more. Only with laughter happiness and Smiles can I truly enjoy the Fruits of my Labor. Smiling is much easier than it is to Fail. Happiness is the remedy that sharpens the taste of any meal. To enjoy Success I must have Happiness. Laughter and Smiling will be the Maiden who serves Me. I will be Happy! I will be Successful! I will be the Greatest Lover in the World.

I Will Smile At The World:

TODAY I WILL MULTIPLY MY PRINCIPLES

Moth Caterpillars touched by the genius of Man becomes Silk. Fields of Clay touched by the genius of Man is built into a Castle. Cyprus Trees touched by the genius of Man is built into a Boat Sheeps Wool touched by the creativity of Man is created into a raiment for a King.

Hence, if it is possible for Moth, Clay, Wood and Wool to have their Values Multiplied a Hundred Folds by Man? Yea! Cannot I do the same with Words of Wisdom that bears my Career for the future? In the name of Grand Style Speech of Poetry Book of Poems?

Today I Will Multiply My Principles One Hundred Folds:

Hence, I am like a Grain of Wheat which faces one of three Futures: The Wheat can be placed in a sack and dumped into a stall and fed too swine. Be ground into Flour and made into Bread. Be placed into the Earth to grow and divide its golden head by producing other Grains from the One.

Hence, I am like Grains of Wheat except with one divine difference: The Wheat cannot choose whether it be fed to swine. Ground for Bread. Planted into the Earth to multiply a hundred folds. I have a choice.

I will not let my Life be fed to Swine.
I will not allow my Life to be ground under the rocks of Failure and Despair. Only to be broken open and devoured by the Wills of others.

Today I Will Multiply My Principles One Hundred Folds:

Hence, to grow and multiply it is necessary to plant Wheat grains into the darkness of the Earth. My Failures, my Despairs, and my Ignorance of my fullest potentials are the darkness which I was born so that I can ripen.

Hence, like Wheat grains that will grow, sprout and blossom only if its nurtured by the Sun, Rain and Wind. I too must nurture my Mind, my Body and my Soul to fulfill my Dreams and my Desires in all my Worldly Affairs. To grow full stature the Wheat must wait on the forces of Nature. I need not wait for the forces of Nature. From Birth. My God have instilled in Me the Power of abilities to control My Own Destiny.

Today I Will Multiply My Principles One Hundred Folds:

Hence, how will I make all my Dreams a reality? First, I will set Goals for each Day, each Week, each Month and each Year for my entire Life. Just as the Rain must fall on the Wheat before it cracks it shall and grow.

Hence, I must also have Plans and Goals before my Life will crystallize. In establishing my goals and objectives in all my Worldly Affairs. I must consider putting forth my best efforts ever. For performing my Plans for the future successfully. Never will I be to concerned about my Goals being too high. For it is better to aim my spear at the Moon yet only striking a rock.

Today I Will Multiply My Principles One Hundred Folds:

Hence, the height of my Goals will not hold me awe. Though, I may stumble often before reaching my Goals and objectives successfully. When I stumble? I will dust myself off with no concerns about falling. I then will continue on my journey for obtaining something essential for the continual existence of better Days to come.

Hence, everyone will stumble now and then before he or she realizes their main purpose or struggles in Life given situations. To Learn is a Struggle, to know is Peace of Mind. Only Worms are free from stumbling. I am not a Worm! I am not an Onion plant! I am not a Sheep! Yea! I am the Greatest Lover in the World. Let others build a cone with their clay. I will build my Career on these Principles.

Today I Will Multiply My Principles One Hundred Folds:

Hence, just as the Sun must warm the Earth to bring forth the Seeds of Wheat to grow. The Words of Wisdom from the Grand Style Speech of Poetry will warm the Life for my Career. And bring forth my fullest potentials and make all my Dreams come true in reality.

Today, I will suppress every action I performed yesterday. I will climb today's Mountain to the utmost of my abilities. Yet, tomorrow I will climb higher than today. My next Mountain will be even higher than tomorrows. Too suppress the deeds' of others are of no importance. Too detain my own deeds are my only concerns for today.

Today I Will Multiply My Principles One Hundred Folds:

Hence, just as the warm Wind guides the Wheat to maturity. The same Wind carries the Words from my Voice to those who will hear my Poems? Once spoken, I will dare not to forget the promises of loving My God, Myself and the Universe righteously. Unless I have lost Faith, Hope and Love for humanity!

Hence, I will act as my own Prophet through utterance, laughter and smiles by sharing my Plans with others; One for All and All for One! Therefore, everyone will know my Dreams. And there will be no escaping from my commitments until my Words of spoken Promises become accomplished Deeds.

Today I Will Multiply My Principles One Hundred Folds:

Hence, I will not commit the terrible crime of aiming to low. I will do the work a lazy person will not do. I will always let my reach exceed my grasp. I will never be content with my performance in the Market Place today. I will always strive to make the next hour better than this hour. I will always announce my goals to my Fellow Men, Women and Children. Yet, I will never proclaim my accomplishments for today. Instead, I will let others approach me with praise. And may I therefore have the knowledge, wisdom and understanding to receive each compliment with Humility?!

Today I Will Multiply My Principles One Hundred Folds:

Hence, one grain of wheat when Multiplied One Hundred Folds will produce a Hundred Stakes. Multiply these a Hundred Folds ten times and they will feed all the cries of Hunger in the World. My human qualities are much more valued than a grain of wheat.

Today I Will Multiply My Principles One Hundred Folds:

Henceforth, when my deeds are done properly?! I will do them, again and again. Then throughout the World. There will be astonishment and wonder about my greatness. As the spoken Words of Wisdom from my Grand Style Speech of Poetry is fulfilled in Me. They will become accomplished deeds by Me. As the Greatest Lover in the World godly.

Today I Will Multiply My Principles One Hundred Folds:

I WILL SHOUT FOR THE ROOF

My Dreams are worthless. My Plans are unimportant. My goals are impossible. All of my Principles are of no Value unless they are followed by Action.

I Will Shout For The Roof:

Henceforth, there have never been a Map, however, carefully detailed which carried its own over every inch of ground without execution. Never has there been a Parchment of Law, however, fair it maybe that have prevented a single crime. Never has there been a Poem regardless of how professionally it was written. That have earned one Penny and produced Words of acclamation.

Action alone is the tinder which ignites a Map, Parchment of Law, Plans, Dreams, Goals and my Poems into a living force. Action is the food and drink that will nourish my Success.

I Will Shout For The Roof:

The Procrastination that has held me back was born in fear. Today, I recognize this as my character defects within my personality. When the Principles from the depths of all those courageous hearts before me Jived not in fear. Today, I realize that I must conquer fear. I therefore must always Act without hesitation wisely, in order to succeed. The flutters in my heart will vanish when I take action to reduce the Lion of terror to an Ant of equanimity.

I Will Shout For The Roof:

I will always remember the Lessons about the Firefly. Who gives off Light only when its Wings are in Motion. My Actions will be like the Fire fly. Even in the Day Time my glow will be seen in spite of the Sun Light. Let others be like the Butter fly who Preens its Wings. As it depends on the charity of the Flowers for survival. When the Fireflies action in motion brightens the World.

I Will Shout For The Roof:

Henceforth, I will not avoid my Task for today. By changing my plans until tomorrow. Tomorrow may never come. I Will Act now. Even though my Actions may not bring happiness or success for today. But it is better to Act and Fail, then, not Act and Flounder. In truth, happiness may not be the fruit plucked by all my Actions. Yet, without Action all fruits on the vines will die.

I Will Shout For The Roof! I Will Shout For The Roof! I Will Shout For The Roof! I Will Act Now!

Hence, I will repeat these Words each day and every day again and again until they become like a habit of Breathing. And as instinctive as blinking my eye lids. With these Words I will discipline myself to perform every Act that is necessary to achieve success honestly. As I meet every challenge that a coward will avoid fearfully.

I Will Shout For The Roof:

Hence, when I awaken each morning I will recite these Words and leap from my bed while a lazy person yet sleeps another hour. When I enter the Market Place I will immediately confront my first prospect while a procrastinator ponders on the possibility of rebuttal. When I am faced with closed doors I will knock While a person with uncertainty waits outside with fear and trepidation.

I Will Shout For The Roof:

When I am confronted with Temptation for evilness I will instantly remove myself from Harms Way. When I am tempted to quit today and begin tomorrow I will Act promptly to consummate yet another exchange of Love for Spiritual Growth in Fellowship.

I Will Shout For The Roof:

Only Action determines my value in the Market Place. To Multiply my values I must Multiply my Actions. I will walk where a coward fear to walk. I will Work when the lazy seeks rest. I will Speak when the procrastinator remains silent. I will call on ten who will purchase my goods while the person with uncertainty makes grand plans to call on just one. I will say it is done before the person with low self esteem say I am ready.

I Will Shout For The Roof:

Today, is all I have to prove my worthiness. Tomorrow is the day reserved for the lazy. I am not Lazy. Tomorrow is the day when the evil becomes good. I am not Eviler. Tomorrow is the day when the weak becomes Strong. I am not weak. Tomorrow is the day when the coward becomes fearless. I am not a Coward.

I Will Shout For The Roof:

Hence, when the Lion is hungry it eats. When the Eagle is thirsty it drinks. Unless they both act they will perish.

I Will Shout For The Roof:

Henceforth, I am hungry for Success. I am thirsty for happiness and peace of mind. Unless I acted now I will perish in a Life of failure, misery and sleepless nights. I will command myself to act on the Principle of Self Determination. And I will obey my own commandments.

36

Success will not wait for anyone. If I delay my actions I will be dethroned from my principles. And they will be lost to me forever. This is the time. This is the Place. I am the person. I Am The Greatest Lover In The World.

I Will Shout For The Roof:

THE SPIRIT OF GOD WILL GUIDE ME

Henceforth, who is of so little Faith in a moment of disaster have not called too their God? Who have not cried out for help when danger beyond ones normal experiences have occurred?! Yesterday, Today and Tomorrow?!

The Spirit Of God Will Guide Me:

Hence, where has this deep instinct come from which escapes our mouths? From any living species in moments of excitement or despair?! Move your hands in haste in front of someone's eyes and their eyelids will blink. Tape the knees of a person's leg and it will automatically jump. Confront anyone with dark horror and his or her instinctive reactions would be Oh My God! From the same impulse.

The Spirit Of God Will Guide Me:

My Life does not have to be filled with any religious practice in order for me to recognize this extraordinary mystery of Nature. All of Gods' creations were born with this foreknowledge from birth. Where we must use our natural senses and abilities to know when one needs help. Personally or otherwise. Why do we possess this splendid inclination from nature? Is it that this is a form of cries? Or Prayer? Why would it be necessary in our wordly affairs to have the Laws of God to Governed our Lives? And Mankind and every animal species instinctively to cry out or pray for help?

Unless some superior force have thought out a reason that a cry should be heard by some higher being? Who have the authority to answer our cries? I Will Pray. My cries will always be for Guidance.

The Spirit Of God Will Guide Me:

Hence, as a child I never understood the Power of Prayer. Nor did I foresee the rewards. that came from Praying consciously. Even though sub-consciously my instincts are about doing the right things. But my childhood environment were mostly about playing games. Good & Bad!

The Spirit Of God Will Guide Me:

Prayer were never explained in details as Paying Ties Too God. As We Ask So Shall We Receive. From the God of Your Understanding. Today, I Pray to my God jehovah; in the Person of Jesus Christ, the living god, the Universal Mind. For guidance to succeed in all my Worldly Affairs.

Spiritually, Physically and Financially. As I strive in all my endeavors with the communion of faith, hope and love. With the Laws of God being my guide as I Work toward controlling my own destiny successfully.

The Spirit Of God Will Guide Me:

Henceforth, today I do not Pray for food, clothing or shelter. Because my God have supplied me with His Knowledge, Wisdom and Understanding programmed into my instincts. Based on plans of action to accomplish anything essential for the continuation of my Well Being in the Wilderness of my society godly.

The Spirit Of God Will Guide Me:

Nor will I Pray for the delivery of patty victories in Worldly Affairs that is controlled by materialistic things. I Pray only for guidance. That my God will give me the Power in my abilities to acquire the necessities for Survival of the Fittest, spiritually, physically and financially . . . With His Knowledge of Changing the Things I Can Wisely.

The Spirit Of God Will Guide Me:

In truth, my Prayers and cries will always be answered. Yesterday, Today and Tomorrow. Whether the guidance I seek is asked for or knocked for? Will always come or not come?! My Prays and my cries have been answered. In the principle of Collective Work and Responsibility. If a Child seeks attention for food, clothing or warmth from its guardian?! And the mother, father or the person legally entrusted with its care are not forth coming?! Haven the Child's Cries been answered?

The Spirit Of God Will Guide Me:

Henceforth, my prayer for guidance shall be prayed for in this manner, as the Greatest Lover In The World:

"The Spirit of My Father, Lord God, Jehovah! Creator of the Heaven, the Earth and the Universe! With its Principles of Life, I Honor Your Holy Name! I Ask! that Your Kingdom of Mercy will come now! May Your Will be done here on Earth just as it is in Heaven? Give me my Food again today as usual, and forgive me for my bad habits, sin and evilness?! Of lust, greed, anger, attachment, ego, smoking, cursing, lying and fornication! just as I am trying to forgive those who've committed ill wills against me! don't bring me into temptation but deliver me from the evil ones!"

"The Spirit of my Father, Lord God, Jehovah! Creator of all people, places and things in the material world, with its Principles of Life! Grant me peace and serenity to accept the things I cannot change! Give me courage, awareness, wealth, good health, free will, self determination, patience and opportunities to change the things I can! Bless me with knowledge, wisdom and understanding to know the difference between the things I cannot change and the situations I can! In Your Holy Name let there be Light!"

"My lord hood! My masculine title of nobility of a man with renowned power and authority to control my own destiny! My Body! My abode and home of the Spirit of my Father, Lord God, Jehovah! in the Person of Jesus Christ! My temple! My worshiping place in union with my ancestors from the Spirit of my Father, Lord God, Jehovah! in the Person of Jesus Christ, the living god!

"My kingdom! My heart is ruled by the Spirit of my Father, Lord God, Jehovah! in the Person of Jesus Christ, the living god! the Spirit that is dominant within me!"

"My way of life! I must evaluate my life, the truth and the way everyday in oneness with the Spirit of my Father, Lord God, Jehovah! My Spiritual journey begins at the Soles of my Feet, to the Crown of my Head! in Harmony with the Spirit of my Father, Lord God, Jehovah! in the Person of Jesus Christ,! True Self-Knowledge, the living god! let there be Light!"

"The Spirit of my Father, Lord God, Jehovah! I Pray! and I Thank You! for this glorious and beautiful Day! __d __m __y? I Pray! that you will bless me with more glorious and beautiful Days ahead in Your Holy Name!"

"The Spirit of my Father, Lord God, Jehovah! I Pray! that You will grant peace and serenity to those who seek Your Holy Name, to accept the things they cannot change, in Your Holy Name?! My Father, Lord God, Jehovah! I Pray! that You will bless those who seek Your Holy Name?! with knowledge, wisdom and understanding, to change the things they can, in Your Holy Name?! My Father, Lord God, Jehovah! I Pray! that You will bless Me! with courage, awareness, wealth, good health, free will, self determination, patience and opportunities to change the things I can?!

In Your Holy Name! let there be Light!!! in lust, greed, anger, attachment, ego, smoking, cursing, lying and fornication!!! Also, my Father, Lord God, Jehovah! Let there be Light!!! in sacrifice, charity, self-control, discrimination and humility, against, smoking, cursing, lying and fornication!!! In Your Holy Name!!! In the Person of Jesus Christ, the living god, the Universal Mind!

Aman:

The Spirit Of God Will Guide Me:

DISGRACE IN THE HUMAN RACE

Conflict lingers on and on; man against man to control the material things in the world for their very own. People over here against people over there; men killing one another without any care.

Disgrace In The Human Race:

What is all the hype about that must be shown; when God Himself is King of the Throne. Is it lust, greed, anger, attachment or ego; causing problems in homes, schools, neighborhoods and people on the go. Could it be there isn't enough material wealth in the world to fulfill our needs; maybe it is the same old mind-set all about greed.

Disgrace In The Human Race:

Without a doubt, there is plenty of space on Earth for all of Mankind; too prosper, succeed and be happy without disrespect and dying. Living life day by day is short enough as it is; no need for noise about this religion of any other nation because their agendas are hide. Our biggest problem among ourselves are the lack of cooperative economics cooperation; people are starving, living in the streets, many of them are in need of a donation.

Disgrace In The Human Race:

Every group of people should have their own unions to pay their dues with a cost; being ready, willing and able to follow their leaders with honor as their boss. Having faith, hope and love in true leadership that will last; focusing on collective work and responsibility as a principle for the mass.

Hard work with good business sense; should be the main objective and not straddling the fence. Some members will act like crabs in a barrel by fooling around; as some try to pull themselves up while others try to pull them down.

Disgrace In The Human Race:

God bless the child with his or her very own in the world; fathers and mothers who strive to take care of their little boys and girls. Self employment with reliable friends; is a good thing when they all stick & stay too the end.

Education based on true self-knowledge will help everyone to know about each other's race; being very helpful when studying our own individual case. Learning and understanding knowledge about this or that subject will seem hard; it is all about building a true and lasting government of God.

Gang related activities seem to be out of control; would this have anything to do with respect, money and power, or, the real story have yet to be told. Some group members possess money with an attitude that this is the real deal; never making sound investments instead they just buy automobiles. Expressing no-none-sense words to say that he; I am making money, money do not make me.

Disgrace In The Human Race:

When every penny is used up and it's time for a new start; some people get angry with the other man who is got it going on cause he want give them a job. Working to support oneself and not depending on others; using your own common sense and not relying on your brothers.

The new millennium has come· for all people to get on their feet; giving our children extracurricular activities for keeping up the beat. Pulling our resources together to help those doing their best; good examples from true leadership will eliminate Disgrace In The Human Race for the rest.

WHEN JESUS VISITS YOU

Jesus comes to your house to spend a day or two; He comes unexpectedly what would you do?

Give Him your best room as an honored guest; or nothing at all cause you yourself have even less?

Overly excited He's visited your home today; offering Him every kind of food as He stay?

You opened the door and to your surprise; He stood right before you with a very bright smile.

Not knowing exactly what to say or do; you begin thinking to yourself is this really true?

Your clothing being the same as they was the day before; thinking again to yourself how in the world was I suppose to know?

Greeting Him would you hug, kiss and shake His hand; or treat Him with disrespect like you did your brother man?

Grooving to your favored beat; keyed-up and so off the hook you forget to offer Him A seat?

Jesus were now there with you; do you keep on talking the same talk you are use to?

Would you want Jesus to meet your very close friends; or hope they stay away until His visit ends?

It would be interesting to know the things you will say or do; if Jesus Christ in person came to spend some time with you?

GETTING OLD BLUES

A few days ago I received a letter from an old friend; talking about how things have really changed from then. My lady friend wrote her letter in this way; this is what she had too say.

Dearly beloved OT!

This is just a few words of wisdom to you from me. Remember always that we older folks are worth a fortune in gold; I am a living witness with a true story that must be told.

With silver in our hair and gold in our teeth; stones in our kidneys, gas in our stomachaches and lead in our feet.

I have become a little bit older since we saw each other last; some changes have come into my life from the past.

Honestly I have become quite a frivolous little girl; now days I am seeing five gentlemen everyday who gives me the world.

My first gentlemen is will power; as soon as I wakeup he helps me out of bed on the hour. Then my second gentlemen is john; after seeing him I am on the run. My third gentlemen is Charlie horse; taking up lots of my time with his loud noisy.

When Charlie leaves then arthur ritis shows up and stay with my all day; who do not like playing around he takes me all the way. After such a busy day with those four on my tray; I be so tired OT that I am glad to go to bed with ben gay.

What an exciting life I have!

Your Beloved Friend,

Caniget A. Witness

PS: The other day my Preacher came to visit me; he said that at my age I should be thinking about the hereafter life to see. I told him oh I do all the time; with the Getting Old Blues I am doing just fine. No matter where I am; in the hair parlor, upstairs, in the kitchen, in the basement or on-my-knees I always ask myself now what am I hereafter Sam?

HI TEC<>KNOW-LEDGE

You ever wonder what it would be like to Pray to God. If He decide to have Voice/Email installed in this new age of Hi Tec<>Know-Ledge? Imaging yourself Praying only to hear an operator with the following reply.

Thank you for calling Heaven1
For English? Press 1!
For Spanish? Press 21
For all other Languages? Press O!

Please select one of the following options.
Press 1 for your requests!
Press 2 for Thanksgiving!
Press 3 for Complaints!
Press 4 for all other Inquiries!

I am sorry! All of our Angels and Saints are busy helping other Sinners right now. Please remember your Prayers are very important to Us. And we will answer your Prayer in the order it was received. Please have patience and stay on the line.

If you would like to Pray directly?
Press 1 for Our Father Lord God Jehovah!
Press 2 for Our Lord God Jesus Christ, the living god, our universal mind!
Press 3 for your Prays to be answered by the Holy Spirit!

If you would like to have Bible Verses read to you while you are holding-on? Press 4!

To find a Loved one whom you believe has been assigned to Heaven? Press 51 (entered with his or her social security number then please press the pound sign). Note: If by chance you received a negative response? Please hang-up and dial the area code 666.

For your personal reservation to heaven's gate enter J.O.H.N. followed by the numbers 3-1-6.

If you become bored while waiting and would like some answers to nagging questions about the age of the Earth, Dinosaurs or life on other planets and where Noah's Ark is located? Please wait until you arrive! Our computer shows according to your email you have Prayed today. So please hang-up and try again tomorrow.

And please remember. Our Office will be Closed for the weekend to observe a special religious holiday. If by chance you are calling after hours and need emergency assistance? Please contact your local Pastor. Better yet. Please email our office at: <Ihavenotprayedtoday@GOD.com>. We will response to your message at our earliest convenience.

Thank you for calling today! May you have a Blessed and Heavenly Day! And a better Tomorrow!

Yours Truly,

HiTech<>Know-Ledge Praying Voice/Email To God for the Future.

ONE-TWO-FOUR-SEVEN

One Two Four &Seven; Universal Principles in numbers that God designed in Heaven. He assigned them to yours truly; for striving and working toward every material and spiritual gift, reward and blessing that are due me.

Knowledge is my first Principle of His Divine Key; using the proper application for True Self Knowledge I will know Him godly.

Wisdom is my second principle for His Righteous Door; learning from my experiences through my life journey of yesterday, today and tomorrow His Commandments I will Know.

Culture is my fourth principle of His human creation; no man, woman, child or animal species are exempted from His Laws of Nature.

God is my seventh principle of His Perfect Number in humanity; every man, woman, child, animal and element in the universe must pay-ties to Him in serenity.

Now that you have been informed about my Universal Principles of the numbers One, Two, Four and Seven assigned to me from birth; working in collective work and responsibility to build a Spiritual Community here on Earth.

Power is our fifth principle that God have instilled in us all; with the abilities of Free Will too choose between right and wrong.

Build & Destroy is our eighth principle for balance; with Gods' knowledge, wisdom and understanding He will help us All with this challenge.

Born is our ninth principle for re-birth; every man, woman and child must have True Self Knowledge for your own Self Worth.

Well! I guess it is time to finish this poem and go to bed; so that you the reader can think by using your own head. Good Night! And Sweet Dreams!

UNCLE BUD'LEE

Uncle Bud'Lee was a real good man too see;
he was a Spiritual Angle to me.

Uncle Bud'Lee was my Mother's Brother;
he was that also to others.

Uncle Bud'Lee was thought of as a bad person by a few;
cause they did not know him like I do.

Uncle Bud'Lee had no children I knew;
stories was told he had plenty of women he went through.

Uncle Bud'Lee was like a hermit it seem;
traveling from here to there and just living his dream.

Uncle Bud'Lee came into my life when I was a child;
living with Mommer & Popper for quite a while.

Uncle Bud'Lee suddenly disappeared one day;
fifty years later I still do not know which way.

My Uncle Bud'Lee I guess have returned back where it starts;
My love, faith, hope and Prayers for Uncle Bud'Lee is that he has risen back into the Care of God.

GOD'S LOVE

God's Love endureth forever, what a wonderful thing too know; when the tides of life run against you, and your spirit is down-cast and low!!!

God's Love.

God's kindness is ever around you always ready too freely impart; strength too your faltering spirit cheer too your lonely heart!!!

God's Love.

God's presence is ever beside you, as near as the reach of your hand; you have but too tell Him your troubles there is nothing He won't understand!! !

God's Love.

And knowing God's Love is unfailing, and His Mercy unending and great; you have but too trust in His Promise, God comes not too soon or too late!!!

God's Love.

So wait with a heart that is patient for the goodness of God too prevail; for never do Prayers go unanswered and His Mercy and Love never fail!!!

God's Love.

ANYWAY

Any Way people are, unreasonable, illogical and self-centered and so-on; Love them Any Way, for their own self-harm!!!

If you do good people will accuse you with self-fish ulterior motives—do good Any Way!!!

If you are successful, you will win false friends, and true-enemies, succeed Any Way!!!

Honest & frankness makes you vulnerable, be honest & frank Any Way!!!

The good you do today, will be forgotten tomorrow, do good Any Way!!!

The biggest people with the biggest ideas can be shot-down, by the smallest people with the smallest-minds, Think big Any Way!!!

People favor under-dogs, but follow only top-dogs,

fight for some under-dogs Any Way!!!

What you spend years building, maybe destroyed over-night, build Any Way!!!

Give the World the best you have, and you will get kicked-in-the-teeth, Give The World The Best You Have—Any Way!!!

SHADOWS OF THE PYRAMIDS

The World cast its Shadows down on all the Pyramids, on Earth; today, we will not fail like others, from our birth.

In our abilities, we now hold the charts too guide us through each storm; too shores of success, and happiness without harm!!!

Failure, is no longer the payment for our struggles day-in & day-out; our journey today, will make yesterdays failures seem but a dream, from our birth, today, here on earth, without a doubt!!! Shadows Of The Pyramids.

The Universal Laws have not made any provisions for our bodies too tolerate pain; nor, has any of Gods Universal Laws made any preparation for our careers too suffer failure, by His Name; failure, like pain; is alienated from our lives like rain!!! Shadows Of The Pyramids.

In the past, we accepted Failure, just as we have accepted Pain; but today, we reject both, fully dosed—with knowledge, wisdom & understanding gained!!! Shadows Of The Pyramids.

GARDEN OF HASTINESS

Hence, even the golden apple in the Garden Of Hastiness will seem no more than your just reward; Time, teaches all people, places, things & animals, that there is no greater Power, than the Lord!!! Garden Of Hastiness.

You & I must submit to the Laws of Nature, to live a Happy & Successful Life; something essential for the continual existence of Life itself, as we roll the dices!!! Garden Of Hastiness.

You or I may not have the luxury of eternity; within our allotted Time, we must Learn to practice the art of patience, Gods Universal Laws are never acts in Hasty!!! Garden Of Hastiness.

Creation of the Olive Tree, has a one hundred-year-old-birth; an Onion Plant, is old in nine-weeks, whose deterioration is first!!! We have lived as Onion Plants, humanly; that, has not pleased our desires of becoming godly!!! Garden Of Hastiness.

Today, you & I must become the best of Olive Trees; in truth, we must become the Greatest Lovers in-the-world, with godly deeds!!! Garden Of Hastiness.

DIVINE TASK OF GREATNESS

How will I accomplish this Divine Task; too begin with, consciously, I have not the Knowledge, Wisdom, Understanding & Experience to achieve such Greatest that will last!!! Divine Task Of Greatness.

Blindly, I have stumbled into ignorance, and fallen into pools of self-pity; when in truth, the answers to all my problems lies in simplicity!!! Divine Task Of Greatness.

I must follow the narrow-path of the chosen few; wisely, ignoring the wide-road of the fools, whose traffic-signs reads—cannot go through!!! Divine Task Of Greatness.

Today, the beginning of my mission, is to commence my journey un-afraid; with the weight of necessary experience, and the handicap of meaningless knowledge, wisdom & understanding as my aide!!! Divine Task Of Greatness.

God, My Universal-Mind, Super-Consciously, has already supplied Me with necessary knowledge, and natural-instincts superior to any beast around me; for personal-success, happiness, and peace-of mind, in serenity!!! Divine Task Of Greatness.

The value of Experience is usually over-rated by old-men, who nod wisely, but speak foolishly; when experience teaches thoroughly, yet, the reasons behind its wisdom devours the years of men constantly!!!

To earn this special Knowledge, Wisdom & Understanding of becoming godlike; the Principles of Sacrifice, Charity, Self Control, Discrimination & Humility must be confessed in prayer, each night!!! Divine Task Of Greatness.

Death, commonly finds True-Wisdom wasted on dead-men; true-wisdom from experience is comparable to fashion—an action proven successful today—will be un-workable, and not practiced at tomorrow's end!!! Divine Task Of Greatness.

SPOKEN WORD

Only Principles Endure; today, I possess these Laws in my Poetry too help me mature!!!

That will guide me toward Greatness contained in the Spoken Word of each Poem; teaching me too prevent Failure, which is just a state-of-mind, I must Learn!!!

Two among one-thousand wise-men will define success with the same Words; each Spoken Word should carry a message with a healing-force that should be heard!!!

Failure is always described but one-way; its Mans lack of abilities to reach his or her Goals, in real-live situations for a better Day!!!

In reality, the only difference between those who failed, and those who succeed; exist in ones unbalanced habits based on Need vs. Greed!!!

Good Habits are the key to Success; when you are at your Best!!!

Bad Habits, are the un-locked-doors of Failure for many; with a craving-desire for anything as long as the Spoken Word is based on plenty!!!

As a Child, I was a slave too my impulses childishly; as an Adult today, I am a slave too my Bad Habits, foolishly!!!

In the past, I surrendered my Free Will too the years of accumulated habits sadly; past deeds have marked-out-a-path, which threatens to imprison my future madly!!!

Today, I must build my disciplines with Good Habits, and destroy the Bad-Habits from then; rescuing myself from Sin!!!

How will I accomplish this difficult feat?! It is suggested—with Faith in each Poems Spoken Word on a regular beat; this will regulate my abilities from suffering Failure—without defeat!!! Spoken Word.

HIDDEN SECRETS TOO LONGER LIFE

Herein, lives the Hidden Secrets Too Longer Life for every Man, Woman & Child, victoriously; as these Words of Wisdom is repeated daily, becoming apart of Ones Universal Mind Super Consciously, in reality!!!

This mysterious Force which never Sleeps within You; but makes Us acted in ways You & I never dreamed too be true!!! Hidden Secrets Too Longer Life.

As this knowledge, wisdom & understanding is consumed by your mysterious-gods-mind, consciously; you begin to awaken each morning with a new vitality, you have never known before truly!!!

Your vigor increases, your enthusiasm rises; your desire to greet the World, over comes every fear you have never known at Sun Rise!!! Hidden Secrets Too Longer Life.

There are times when you find yourself acting & reacting toward every situation confronting you; respond correctly with true-self-knowledge, you will then become more happier, than you thought was impossible for you to do!!! Hidden Secrets Too Longer Life.

Any Act with Practice becomes easier to perform whenever it is practiced regularly; when an Act becomes easy through constant repetition it is a pleasure to perform sincerely!!! A New & Good Habit Is Born!!!

It is in Your Gods Nature too represent the standards of Good Behavior; as you represent Goodness, and it becomes a slave, since it is a gracious Habit, this is Your Free Will with True Labor!!! Hidden Secrets Too Longer Life.

NEW LIFE

Today, you begin a New Life; making a solemn oath to yourself with the best of your ability, that you will live it honestly without strife!!!

Not allowing nothing too retard your growth & development for a better New Way of Life; by not losing a day from your lessons for building Positive Habits, and destroying Negative Habits that's not nice!!! New Life.

Any day wasted cannot be retrieved, nor, can you substitute another for it; you should not break your habit of studying your lessons daily, don't quit!!! New Life.

In truth, the few moments spent studying your lessons each day; is just a small price to pay for the Happiness & Success gained from your own way!!! New Life.

Never allow the brevity of each habit, nor, the simplicity of words too cause yourself to treat the message in your lessons lightly; thousand-of grapes are pressed to fill only one-jar with wind, righteously!!! New Life.

The skins & pulp are tossed too the Birds too eat; historically, these grapes of Knowledge & Wisdom was passed-down from your Ancestors, has been filtered, and tossed into-the-wind for you as a treat!!! With only the pure-truth laying distilled in the Words too come!!! New Life.

Eat as instructed, and waste not one-crumb; these Bread Crumbs are tokens of success, you should eat & share them, like the Sounds of music from your Drums!!! New Life.

Today, Your Old Skin has become dust; walk-tall among all-the-manners of your Fellow Men, Women & Children, with Faith, Hope, Love & Trust!!! One For All & All For One!!! New Life.

THE SPEECH OF POETRY, BOOK OF POEMS,

are my New Beginning in the Life of something essential for the continual existence of Poetry itself, for generations too come. As a Poet, (with an attitude), expressing my most deepest thoughts about living life-on-life terms!!! One Poem at-a-time!!! With Faith, Hope and Love for my God, Myself and the Universe!!! As I communicate with my true feelings, emotions and mannerism based on the Title of each Poem. Please Note: SPEECH OF POETRY, BOOK OF POEMS, is a revised edition of the Grand Style Speech Of Poetry, printed in the year of 2007 . . . with the same concept in mind!!! Too Learn is a Struggle;

Too Know is Mind-At-Peace!!!